The Teen Handbook
A Bit of Help with Life

Kimberly Willis, PhD
Life Dynamics Books

Life Dynamics Books

This publication contains the opinions and ideas of its author. It is intended to provide helpful and informational material on the subjects addressed in the publication. It is sold with the understanding that the author and publisher are not engaged in rendering medical, health, or any other kind of personal professional services in this book. The reader should consult his or her medical, health, or other competent professional before adopting any of the suggestions in this book or drawing inferences from it.

The author and publisher specifically disclaim all responsibility for any liability, loss, or risk, personal or otherwise, which is incurred as a consequence, directly or indirectly, of the use and application of any of the contents of this book.

For Rosie and Molly, my teenagers.

Contents...

SECTION 1
ABOUT THIS BOOK

The situation...

So here you are,
    you are not a little child
        even though your parents are convinced you still are.

You choose what you want to wear.

You have your own friends, probably your own phone.

You have your own money - though probably not as
much as you would like.

You have to face many new and sometimes stressful situations.

It can sometimes feel that you have to face these things alone.

This book will help you to cope...

You can use this book by yourself or you can work through it with someone.

You can read it back to front, from the middle out or upside-down.

This is your book...

This is your life...

How this book works...

Find the Section that you need.

Each section contains all you need to deal with the issue that is causing your problems - it might be sleep, feeling anxious or getting through exams.

If you need help with more than one issue you will find some of the exercises repeated in each section.

Tapping

In each section there is an exercise, which involves tapping on certain points on your face. Doing this helps your body to shift stuck emotions - these trapped feelings can stop you from feeling more positive and confident.

You can repeat the tapping once or twice with a few days in-between - this will help that stuck feeling shift.

Other Exercises

Along with tapping there are other exercises, which are all easy to use. Some of these like 'Planted Feet' can help you when you are in a specific situation.

Other exercises - like 'A Film of You', can be done at home, in preparation for a certain event - like giving a talk.

Remember - you were not born with these issues; they are not part of you.

Just as they came along they can now go away!

SECTION 2
Finding Your Confidence

I want to
run away

Talks

Meeting
people

Everyone is
looking at me

I feel
sick

I can't get
the words out

New
places

Presentations

My hands
are shaking

I'm not good
enough

Help, I need more Confidence!

Remember...

You are not alone.

Even the most confident looking person in the world will have felt nervous at some point in their life.

You can **learn** how to feel confident.

That's what they did.

Something Happened That Took Your Confidence...

Just because something happened once doesn't mean that it will happen again. The past does not predict the future.

Doing this exercise once or twice will help your mind break free from that bad memory.

Tap 8 times on each point with two fingers while repeating the statement below over and over again:

Something happened that took my confidence, and I am ok.

Do this when something that happened keeps worrying you - this will help you let go of those negative thoughts.

A Film of You...

Is there an event coming up that you want to feel confident for?
Go through this exercise a few times before that event and you will find yourself feeling more confident.

Creating your film:

Read through this then give it a go.

- Imagine there is a TV in front of you.

- Playing on this TV is a film of that day in your future.

- Imagine that you could see yourself before the event, getting ready.

- See yourself going to the event.

- Now you can imagine that you see everything going well, imagine where you are, see the people around you.

- Everything goes just as you would like it to.

- You feel good, look happy, confident.

- You return home, happy, it went well and you are smiling and feeling good.

You might find it helpful to close your eyes, or to stare at a blank space on the wall in front of you.

This is great preparation for giving a talk - do this a couple of times in the days leading up to the talk and you will find yourself feeling much more confident on the day.

Tapping Your Way into Confidence...

This exercise will help you feel more confident about an upcoming event.

Think about what you need confidence for - get those nervous feelings up - then start tapping.

Tap 8 times on each point with two fingers while repeating the statement below over and over again:

Even though I am nervous of - (giving a talk, meeting new people, walking into a room) .... I am ok.

Finally gently tap all over the top of your head with your fingertips like raindrops.

You can do this exercise just before an event, and if you need to, you can do it on the days leading up to that event.

Breathing out butterflies...

So, today is the day you want to feel confident.
You wake up and find your stomach feels strange.

Here's how to get rid of those butterflies:

Place your fingertips on the area just under your collarbone halfway between the centre of your chest and shoulder.
Take some deep breaths while gently pressing this point.

Now:

Focus on that feeling in your stomach.

Now imagine that feeling in your stomach has a colour.

What colour would it be?

If it had a shape - what shape would it be?

How big is that feeling?

What do you imagine would be a better colour?

Close your eyes and imagine it easily changing colour.

What do you imagine would be a better shape?

Close your eyes and imagine it easily changing shape.

Now its changing shape and becoming smaller and smaller.

Take in a deep breath and you will find you can just breathe out that feeling, letting it go.

Notice how much better you are now feeling.

This is a great exercise to do when you are getting ready for the day. Just taking a moment or two in your bedroom to do this will help you to feel calm and confident.

Release That Negativity...

When you are nervous your body releases chemicals into your muscles, which build up over time.

Releasing this build up of chemicals will help you feel more positive.

Stretching will help release those negative chemicals:

Take some deep breaths while doing this exercise.

- Stand up.

- Stretch your arms above your head. Now stretch your arms over to one side, hold for one breath - then stretch over to the other side.

- Look up and stretch your hands as far back as it is comfortable, take a deep breath then move your hands back upright.

- Gently lower your hands and slowly bend over, again as far as is comfortable, touching the floor if you can.

- Now roll gently up, making sure you use your stomach muscles.

- Standing upright start swinging your arms from side to side - keeping your feet still. Slowly begin to lift your arms while still swinging from side to side from waist height then to shoulder height. And keep swinging from side to side while slowly lowering your arms.

- Take a deep breath and smile.

You can do this exercise whenever you need to. It doesn't have to be for a specific event - it will help you lower your nervousness and allow your confident self through!

That Dosey Time...

Doing this will set you up for a great day.

You have just woken up.

You are still in bed, warm and comfortable, snuggled down under the covers, you could drift back off to sleep.

This is your POWER TIME.

Suggestions you make to your brain at this time will have a powerful effect.

Imagine the day going well.

Saying to yourself 'I will feel confident all day'.

Close your eyes and just run through how you want your day to go and how you want to feel. You can imagine meeting people, doing all that you need to, looking and feeling confident.

This is such a simple thing to do and it is amazingly powerful. You can get into the habit of doing this most mornings; it will help prepare your mind for a great day.

Creating Your Own Confidence Booster...

This is a fantastic way of giving your confidence a boost wherever you are.

Setting up your confidence booster:

Think about a time when you felt good about yourself. It could be - the day you did well in a spelling test, when you scored a goal, the day you got something you really wanted.

Close your eyes and really think about that moment - where you were, how you felt, feel that good feeling growing inside of you. Imagine you were there again, right now.

Clench your hands into fists and hold that good feeling, feel it growing stronger inside you.

Repeat - to make it even more powerful.

Now when you need a confidence boost - clench your hands and feel that good feeling flow through you, blasting confidence into every part of you.

Set your booster up at home - then when you need a blast of confidence - perhaps when you are going to stand up and talk in front of people - you can use your booster and feel good.

Planted Feet...

This is a great exercise that you can use anywhere. It's easy and effective. It will help lower your nerves and allow your confidence to shine through.

- Take a moment to really notice where your feet are on the ground.

- Sense the weight of your feet on the ground.

- Notice your shoulders; just let them gently relax away from your ears.

- Start to breathe deeply - into the depths of your stomach. So that your breathing moves your stomach in and out. Repeat for a few breaths.

You can use this in combination with the confidence booster to give yourself an amazing boost in self-confidence.

Easy to learn, easy to do - and gives amazing results. You can be in any situation feeling those nerves start and just doing this simple exercise will lower your nerves and allow you to feel more confident.

How will I know if there has been a change?

You will be thinking about an event, waiting to feel nervous, expecting the feeling - and **you will feel ok**.

You will be going to an event - waiting to feel nervous, expecting it - and **you will feel ok**.

You will be at the event - and **you will feel confident**.

Then you will know there has been a change.

The past doesn't predict the future.

**You are a different person today than you were yesterday -
you will be a different person tomorrow.**

Things will get better!!!

*"No one can make you feel
inferior without your consent."*

Eleanor Roosevelt.

SECTION 3
Coping with Stress and Anxiety

My heart is
beating fast

My thoughts are
spinning around

School

Arguments

I am out
of breath

Homework

Friends

I have butterflies
in my stomach

I feel tense

I feel sick

Parents

Exams

My hands
are shaky

I'm stressed out!

What is stress doing to you?

Stopping you from sleeping.
    Making you feel anxious all the time.
Giving you stomach aches.
    Making you bite your nails.
    Making you tired.

Stopping you from being who you want to be.

There are easy techniques that can help you cope with stressful situations.

This section contains a number of different exercises - you can find the ones that work best for you.

You can use each of these exercises when you need them.
Use them separately or all together.

You can learn how to feel calm.

SHOULD • SHOULD • SHOULD • SHOULD • SHOULD • SHOULD

The word *Should* is a stressful word.
>It can make you feel bad.

>>I should have gone to orchestra rehearsal.
>>I should have revised more for English.
>>I should have taken French not German.

Argh!

You cannot change the past.
You can learn from it.
And then let it go.

Look forward to what you now *could* do.
>**Don't let a negative experience affect your future.**

Sometimes you might not realize that you have 'shoulds' spinning around in your brain – stressing you out. When you start to notice them you can begin to let them go.

Tapping Away an Anxious Situation...

Is there a situation that makes you feel anxious every time you are in it?

Like speaking in class or meeting new people.

Going through this exercise once or twice will help you feel much calmer in that same situation.

Tap 8 times on each point with two fingers while repeating the statement below over and over again:

Even though _____ makes me feel anxious I am ok.

Finish by tapping all over the top of your head with your fingertips, like raindrops.

You might find that every time you are called on to speak in class you feel nervous. Thinking about that while tapping through the routine once or twice will help you break free of those stuck feelings.

Rethink Anxiety...

When you feel that anxious feeling - what is your first response?
To run away from it!

Let's rethink Anxiety.

Anxiety = excitement
+ doing something new
+ worry about the unknown

Anxiety is made up of many things — some of them are good things.

So feeling anxious could mean that you are doing something new.

You are expanding your world.

And that's a good thing!

We teach ourselves that any anxiety is a bad thing and that we should run away from it. But life is full of good anxiety - like learning to ride a bike, going on roller coasters etc.

Noisy Breathing...

This is a great way to let go of worries that are building up in your mind. It might look and sound a bit silly - so this could be one to do at home!

Read through and give it a go:

Sit somewhere comfortable - the edge of your bed is a good place.

Now breathe in through your nose and out loudly through your mouth.

Breathing deeply into your belly.

Make this breathing really noisy breathing. Get a real ahhhhh sound coming from the back of your throat as you breathe out.

As you breathe out imagine breathing out worries.

Ahhhh (school work)

Ahhhh (exams)

Ahhh (Spanish test)

As you breathe in you are breathing in calm air, it fills that space inside of you left empty by letting go of those worries.

Do this for a few minutes.

You will find yourself feeling calmer.

This is a great exercise to do when you find you have worries spinning round and round in your head. Doing this will help you let go of them and calm down.

Confidence Booster...

This is a fantastic way of giving your confidence a boost wherever you are. Do the set up at home so you will then have a confidence boost ready whenever you need it.

The set-up, read through and give it a go:

Think about a time when you felt good about yourself. It could be - the day you did well in a spelling test, when you scored a goal, the day you got something you really wanted.

Close your eyes and really think about that moment - where you were, how you felt, feel that good feeling growing inside of you.

Now clench your hands into fists and hold that good feeling, feel it growing stronger inside you.

Repeat this and add another memory to make it even more powerful.

Now when you need a confidence boost - just clench your hands and you will feel that good feeling flow through you, blasting confidence into every part of you.

Use this as you walk into a room full of people and you will find you have more confidence and feel better about yourself.

Make Life About Baby Steps...

Are you getting stressed thinking about all the things you have to do?

You have just started high school

you have to pass all the exams to be able to get into college,
to get a job,
to buy a house,
to get a dog.

STOP

Break it down into baby steps - anyone can do those!

Only think about the next few steps.

Now you can just be thinking about when your next class is, perhaps what you are going to have for lunch.

That you can cope with!

Breaking life down into small baby steps makes everything seem much easier.

Brain Time...

Why not give your hard working brain a rest?

This exercise will help you feel calmer and find life easier to cope with.

Get some brain time:

Close your eyes, or stare straight ahead at one point on a wall.

Scan through your body from the top of your head down to the tips of your toes, just noticing how your body is feeling. Is it comfortable, tired, uncomfortable?

Now notice what mood you are in. Are you stressed, worried, happy? Whatever you are feeling is ok, just check-in and find out.

The next step is to start to focus on your breathing. Breathing slowly in and out, breathing deep into your belly so that your stomach moves as you breathe.

Just focus on your breathing.

Do this for a minute or two.

By building this exercise into your day you will find that you are much calmer and more able to cope with life.

Try gradually increasing the time you spend doing this each day from 2 minutes to 5 minutes then up to 10 minutes over a number of weeks.

Doing this at the end of your day will help lower your stress levels.

Body Time 1...

When you are anxious and stressed your body releases chemicals into your muscles, these build up over time.

Releasing this build up of chemicals will help you feel more positive.

Stretching will help release those negative chemicals:

Take some deep breaths while doing this exercise.

- Stand up.

- Stretch your arms above your head. Now stretch your arms over to one side, hold for one breath - then stretch over to the other side.

- Look up and stretch your hands as far back as it is comfortable, hold for one breath then move your hands back upright.

- Gently lower your hands and slowly bend over, again as far as is comfortable, touching the floor if you can.

- Now roll gently up, making sure you use your stomach muscles.

- Standing upright start swinging your arms from side to side - keeping your feet still. Slowly begin to lift your arms while still swinging from side to side from waist height then to shoulder height. And keep swinging from side to side while slowly lowering your arms.

- Take a deep breath and smile.

When stresses have been building up it is important that you release them - this exercise will help you do this.

Body Time 2...

Exercise helps release the build up of negative chemicals in your body. If you haven't got time to get out and do some exercise try this.

Quick exercise boost:

10 Marches

10 Star Jumps

10 Sit-ups

10 Press-ups

10 Lunges

10 Squat Jumps

Spend a few minutes doing these exercises in any order and you will feel better!

Even a quick burst of exercise will help your body release negative chemicals, helping you to feel better. This is a great thing to do at the end of a stressful day.

Are Your Thoughts Creating More Anxiety?

Take time to notice your thoughts during the day. Thinking negatively will make you stressed and tired.

Your mind is very powerful.

> Thoughts are important.
> They can affect how you feel.
> They can change your body chemistry.

Gaining control over your thoughts will make you happier and healthier.

Start gaining control over your thoughts:

- Are your negative thoughts spinning round and round in your mind?

- Relax your jaw, make sure your teeth aren't clamped together and that your tongue is relaxed.

- Imagine you can put up a big stop sign in your mind, forcing all your thoughts to STOP!

- You can imagine putting your hand up and shouting STOP!

- Now change your thoughts.

Example:

'I'll never get all this work done.'
Now becomes:
'I am working hard, I will get most of my homework done.'

Making a change in your thoughts may seem like hard work at first, you might have had a lot of practice in thinking negatively - but it will get easier and easier.

> *All of us get into the habit of saying negative things to ourselves - taking the time to say positive things can make a huge difference in how you feel.*

Planted Feet...

This technique will help you feel instantly calmer, wherever you are.

Take a moment to really notice where your feet are on the ground.

Sense the weight of your feet on the ground, you can be standing or sitting.

Notice your shoulders let them relax gently down.

Now, notice your breathing.

Start to breathe deeply - into the depths of your stomach. So that your breathing moves your stomach in and out.

Do this for as long as you need to.

This is a great exercise that's so easy you can do it anywhere, even in a classroom and no one will know what you are doing.

A great calmer, you can use this technique if someone or something had stressed you out.

Homework Stress...

A great exercise to do when you are sat at your desk and your homework is stressing you out.

- Place your elbows on the desk in front of you.

- Put your thumbs on your temples and let your fingers lightly rest on your forehead.

- Close your eyes.

- Breathe slowly in and out, breathing deeply into your stomach.

- Allow your shoulders to relax down away from your ears.

- After a couple of minutes, open your eyes.

When you start getting stressed over homework the questions can start to seem harder and harder. Doing this exercise will lower stress and help you to answer with a clear mind.

Your Instant Calmer...

When you find yourself stuck in a stressful situation this is a useful way of quickly calming down.

Rub the area of skin between your finger and thumb - using the finger and thumb of your other hand.

Do this for a minute or two on each hand.

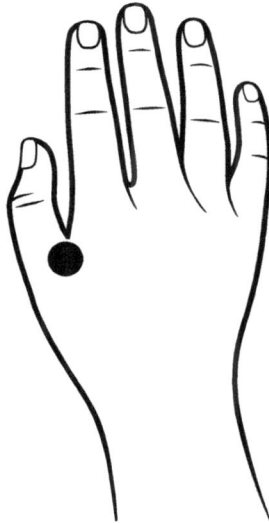

A great calmer – be careful who you teach it to as it's not to be used by pregnant women.

Hug it out...

Your body releases an amazing chemical called oxytocin when you hug and this makes you feel good.

As a teenager you are hugging less than at any other time in your life.

Go on - hug it out!

Even hugging your dog will have a good effect on you!

Emergency Anxiety Help...

Something has happened and now you are completely stressed out.

What can you do?

- Get yourself some space.

- Place one hand on your stomach below your belly button, breathe slowly and deeply to this hand.

- Close your eyes.

- Focus on thinking about a good place - perhaps somewhere where you went on holiday. Just think about being in that place, how it made you feel.

Give yourself a minute or two to do this. Then open your eyes and you will find yourself feeling calmer.

You may have found yourself in a stressful situation - or you might have gotten some news which has stressed you out - doing this will help you calm down.

Are you a God?

No...

So you are not perfect.

So you can make mistakes and be human.

You might not get that grade you want in English.
You might not be able to do a perfect dive.
And that's ok.

Because you are only human.

**Trying to be perfect is tiring.
Being an imperfect Human is wonderful.**

The End of the Day...

You might have had a stressful day, doing this exercise will help you calm down.

It promotes a feeling of relaxation that will help you get to sleep.

- Close your eyes.

- Place one hand over the center of your chest, and place the fingertips of your other hand gently on the top of your spine, at the back of your neck.

- Breathe deeply.

- Open your eyes when you are ready.

Just sit on the edge of your bed and take a minute to do this. Calming down before you get into bed will help you sleep better.

**"If you think you can,
or if you think you can't
you are probably right."**

Henry Ford

SECTION4
Fed up with Feeling Low

I want to hide
away from the world

School

I'm feeling down

What's the point

Bad marks

Homework

I feel sad

I feel like a failure

Friends

Parents

I'm tired

I'm fed up with feeling low

When is a bad mood good?

Sometimes it feels great to be in a bad mood.

You can really get into it. Slam some doors, stomp around and make it known to everyone that you are in a mood.

Well you are a teenager - they expect it!

But sometimes it can be a real pain to be stuck in that bad mood.

You can feel trapped, like you have fallen down a hole of a black mood and can't find your way out.

When this happens it's good to have a way to climb out of that mood and to be able to get on with your life.

What happens when you are feeling down?

Do you do anything .... **No**

Do you have any fun .... **No**

Do you enjoy anything .... **No**

Does everything seem rubbish ....**Yes**

Do you wish you could feel happier ...**Yes**

Do you want some help ....**Yes**

So there you are fed up with being fed up.

This is the right place to start.

Something useful to know:

You can change your mood.

What?

You can change how you are feeling.

You are in charge of how you are feeling.

Your mum can't change your mood.
     Your dad can't change your mood.
          Your brother can't change your mood.
               Your dog can't change your mood.

That means that if you are in a grump or a down mood then you are keeping yourself there.

You are the boss of you.

You just need to learn how to change that mood.

This section will show you some techniques that will help you change your mood.

Some of the excercises in this section are useful to do at home - others will help you be in control of your mood when you are out and about.

Tapping Out of Your Low Mood...

Going through this exercise a couple of times on different days will help your mind start to break free of that low mood.

Tap 8 times on each point with two fingers while repeating the statement below over and over again:

Even though I am feeling down I am ok.

Then tap all over the top of your head with your fingertips - like raindrops.

Doing this exercise when you are feeling low will start to create a change towards a better mood.

Change Your Shape...

When you are feeling sad and low your body responds by curling up and slowing down.

This changes the chemicals in your body.

Your body shape affects how you feel.

How you feel affects your body shape.

You can boost your mood simply by changing your shape.

- Stand up - go on stand up, no one is looking!
- Stretch your hands high up above your head - really stretch up.
- Stretch your fingers apart.
- Look up and now SMILE - show those teeth.
- Take a couple of deep breaths.
- Shake your hands out as you lower your arms.

You might be curled up on your bed, shoulders hunched, head down - just changing your shape will make you feel better. It actually changes the chemicals in your body. This is good to do when you feel yourself standing on the edge of a low mood - one which would be so easy to fall into - doing this might just help you step away from that edge and feel better.

What are you thinking about yourself?

"I'm rubbish"

"I'll never be able to do it"

"Everyone hates me"

Does this sound familiar?

Is thinking this way helpful? Is it making you feel good?

No

So change what you are thinking.

That voice in your head is keeping you down, knocking your self-confidence; it's making you feel bad.

You are no different from anyone else.

This means:

You can achieve whatever anyone else has achieved.

Now say something good to yourself.

Often we block out the good things people say to us – and only hear the bad things – you can now start to hear the good things!

Get Those Voices to be Quiet...

When your mouth and jaw are clamped shut and your brain is a mess of horrible thoughts, your mouth and tongue are making micro-movements - they are saying the words you are thinking.

You can quiet those negative thoughts by:

1.   Unclamping your teeth

2.   Loosening your jaw

3.   Relaxing your tongue

Do this and those horrible voices will get quieter, leaving some room for positive thoughts.

Stopping those thoughts is going to take a bit of practice – after all you have probably been saying horrible things to yourself for a long time. Stopping those thoughts will get easier and easier with practice – and your thoughts will naturally start to become more positive.

What if something goes wrong?
And it makes you feel low...

I can safely predict that you will fail at something.

That something will go wrong.

And that's ok.

You are only human.

You are not perfect.

Even the president of the USA will have failed at something.

Life isn't perfect.

No one is happy all the time - and that's ok.

Michael Jordan, the NBA star, was cut from his high school basketball team.

He said,

"I've failed over and over again in my life. That is why I succeed."

TV, films and adverts make it look like we should be happy all the time. But, in reality, life isn't like that – sometimes things happen that make us feel low – and that's ok, it's normal. Problems only occur when this low feeling goes on and on.

A New Plan...

Do you find that there are certain times of the day or week that you find yourself feeling feel low?

Set up a plan to **now** do something else at this time.

Having a plan makes it easier to change and do something different

When I am	I will now
Feeling low and just sitting in my room	Play the sound track to 'Mamma Mia' really loud
Feeling sad about my hamster	Go for a walk
Fed up with my family	Jump up and down
Feeling grumpy	Wear a hat and paint my nails green

Find a plan that works for you.

Have your plan set out so that when you are feeling low you don't have to think about what to do - you just look at your plan.

Have a piece of paper on your desk at home – you can write your alternative plans on it – then when you find yourself sat alone, feeling sad – you will have an alternative plan you can put into place.

Flip the News Game...

Things happen during the day that might make you feel down - this game can turn this around and make what might have been a mood breaker into something funny.

Bad News	Good News
You are stuck reading this book.	You are feeling better about your life.
There's more to read.	Maybe you will discover something new.
It's raining.	You get to watch a dvd at lunch in school.
You have seen the dvd before.	You get to chat to your friends.

See how many times you can go back and forth with bad news and good news – it can become completely ridiculous!

Boost that Positive Feeling...

This exercise uses acupressure points to boost your mood.

Sit somewhere comfortable, and start breathing deeply.

Using the fingertips of each hand press on the dip below the points on each side of your collarbone, hold this for about five deep breaths.

Now make you hand into a gentle fist and tap on the centre of your chest, your sternum, for 30s.

Finally using your fingertips, tap all over the top of your head, like raindrops.

This is an exercise you can do when you are feeling quiet and thoughtful, perhaps when you are sitting alone in your room – it will help you feel more positive.

Are you looking for proof that it's going to be a bad day?

You wake up - and think it's going to be a bad day.

You bang your toe - now you have proof - it really is going to be a bad day.

Reality Check - the chair was in the way.

Banging your toe doesn't predict how the next 12 hours will go.

Remember

Take a Reality Check!

Sometimes it's like we are wearing glasses that only let us see the negative things. Imagine what life would be like if you could take those glasses off and see all the positive things around you.

Remember to have some fun!

When you are feeling low it's easy to get out of the habit of doing things you enjoy.

Give yourself a few minutes to think about things that you used to enjoy doing - reading, baking, swimming etc.

Do something completely pointless each day - just for fun!

- Paint your toenails in rainbow colours
- Learn how to do a magic trick
- Make paper snowflakes
- Watch a favourite cartoon

I am OK.

A simple thing.

Go-on say it to yourself.

I am OK.

Your Mind and Body are Connected...

So it's not a surprise that what you put into that body of yours will have an effect on how you feel.

Here is a brief guide to how food could be affecting your mood:

1. **White Carbs and Sugars** - potatoes, pasta, rice, sweets and cakes - these give an energy rush - followed by a big energy and mood crash - meaning you will feel low, tired, irritable and hungry.

2. **Aspartame** - this is in many diet foods, it has been shown to drain serotonin levels - this is your brains "feel good" chemical. If you are already feeling low this might make things worse.

3. **Tryptophan** - you need this so that your brain can make the 'feel good' chemical, serotonin. Get it by eating foods high in tryptophan such as - turkey, fish, nuts, eggs, bananas and more. Doing this will help balance your moods and help you feel more positive.

4. **Proteins and Complex Carbs** - eating food high in protein or complex carbohydrates (brown bread, brown rice) gives a gradual rise in blood sugar, without the big crash caused by sugars - this means your mood will be more stable. This will help you maintain your positive mood and your energy.

You can make yourself feel happier just by paying attention to what you are putting in your body.

You will find that by just making a few small changes to your diet you can instantly start to make yourself feel better in mind and body.

What do you control?

Trying to control everything is exhausting it will wear you out and make you feel down.

There are things in your life that you can't control:

Where you live

Who your parents are

Your family

Trying to control these is pointless and will use up all your energy.

Focus your energy on things you can control.

Friends   **Grades**

Mood

Thoughts   **Future**

When you focus your energy on the things that you can change you will find yourself feeling less tired and much more positive. Wasting your energy thinking and worrying about all the things you can't change will leave you drained, tired and low.

Brain Time... The Art of Being Present

Give your hard working brain a bit of a rest and you will feel calmer and more able to cope with life.

Here's how to do it:

Close your eyes, or stare straight ahead at one point.

Scan through your body from the top of your head down to the tips of your toes, just noticing how your body is feeling - is it comfortable, tired, uncomfortable.

Now notice how you are feeling. Are you stressed, worried, happy? Whatever you are feeling is ok - just check-in and find out.

The next step is to start to focus on your breathing. Breathing slowly in and out, breathing deep into your belly.

Do this for a few minutes.

By building this into each day you will find that you are much calmer and more able to cope with life.

Try gradually increasing the time you spend doing this each day from 2 mins to 5 mins then up to 10 mins over a number of weeks.

Doing this before you go to school will give you a great start to the day. It has been shown that doing this regularly helps you feel happier.

It's not fair

Yup.

Ain't that the truth,

Fact: Life isn't fair.

How can you deal with this?

1.   Feel down, hurt by all that life has thrown at you.

OR

2.   Accept it and get over it. Get out there and make something of the life you have.

It's your choice.

I should have ....
I should have ....
I should have ....

This is a killer.

You can't change what has happened.

So drop the 'shoulds' they will make you feel bad, sad and keep you stuck thinking about what could have been.

Nothing is perfect.

Start thinking now about the future.

About what You Could Do.

Let go of the shoulds.

Gale Force Ten!

This exercise will help you let go of some of your worries.

Think about all the things that are bothering you.

Take in a huge deep breath.

Imagine that you are filling that breath with all those thoughts.

Hold it for a moment.

NOW - let that breath go, with a loud puff!

Let go of all those thoughts, imagine just breathing them out.

Now, breathe in a clear calm breath.

Do this when you feel all those worries spinning around in your mind trying to pull you down.

An Act of Kindness...

Want to feel better?

Be kind to someone.

- A small kindness brings you into the world.
- It creates positive links.
- It makes you, and the other person feel better.
- It can be that simple.

You can start with something really small like saying or doing something nice for someone in your family or for a friend.

You are important.

There is only one of you.

There will never be another.

Taking care of You is important.

"People are just about as happy as they make up their mind to be."

Abraham Lincoln

SECTION 5
Learning how to Sleep Again

Find it hard
to concentrate

Get more colds

I'm worrying
about things

My thoughts are
going round and round

Feel low

Feel grumpy

My mind is
spinning

I'm stressed

Feel impatient

Feel moody

I feel tired

I can't sleep

You were born knowing how to sleep...

But sometimes as you get older you might:

- Have problems getting to sleep.
- Have bad thoughts and nightmares that keep you awake.
- Find it hard to get back to sleep after you have woken up.

It's almost as though you have forgotten how to sleep.

Working through the exercises in this section will help your mind and body remember how to sleep.

Sleep is essential...

It's your bodies repair time.

It helps your brain to be well and happy.

Without enough sleep you might find:

- You have more colds.
- Get more spots.
- Find it hard to concentrate.
- Crave sugary foods.
- Feel down and grumpy.

First Simple Steps to a Better Sleep...

Your Bedroom:

Think about energy and chaos, if your room is messy it is a more energetic and chaotic space - tidy it and it will be a calmer place.

Turn off chargers, plugs, screens and computers at bedtime. The electromagnetic radiation generated by these disturbs sleep.

Turn off your mobile phone - or leave it in another room. It emits electromagnetic radiation, which keeps you awake. Even on silent it sends out a pulse every few minutes.

Your Input:

Cut down on tea, coffee and cola drinks - none after mid-afternoon.

Cut down on sugar - it boosts your energy, which stops you sleeping.

Smell is one of your most powerful senses, lavender will help you relax. Have some in your bedroom.

Have a warm bath before bed.

A glass of milk will make you feel sleepy.

Your Body:

During the day get outside and get some natural light. This helps regulate your body's internal clock.

Do some physical exercise during the day; you need to make sure both your mind and body are tired.

If you are worried someone might look at your phone if you leave it in another room – then put a password on it!

Sleepy Foods...

Some foods contain chemicals that promote sleep.

Remember when Peter Rabbit ate all the lettuce and then fell asleep? Well strangely lettuce is one of the foods that promotes sleep - but you might not want to eat it at night - so here are some other foods that will also help:

Almonds   Chamomile Tea

Bananas   Glass of Milk   Oatmeal

Hard-Boiled Egg   Cherries   Whole Grain Cereal

Nightmares...

Nightmares can be very powerful - making you terrified, not wanting ever to close your eyes again.

When you have had a nightmare it can sometimes be very difficult to get back to sleep. This can leave you feeling tired and grumpy the next day. Nightmares usually come along when there are stressful things happening in your life. It's your minds way of dealing with emotions that are trapped inside of you.

Many people keep the fact that they are having nightmares a secret. It's not something that you talk about with your friends.

Sometimes nightmares start when you are having exams, or when there are problems at home or at school – the emotions that you are feeling need a release.

Tapping Free of Sleep Problems...

Working through this exercise a few times on different days will help your mind let go of past sleep problems - preparing the way for a better nights sleep.

Tap 8 times on each point with two fingers while repeating the statement below over and over again:

Even though I have been having problems sleeping, I am ok.

Finish by tapping with your fingertips all over the top of your head like raindrops.

Tapping helps your mind break free from that non-sleeping cycle.

Tennis Ball Relaxation...

Massaging the bottom of your feet releases tensions throughout your body, helping you to get to sleep more easily. Try doing this exercise before going to bed.

Find a tennis ball.

Sit on a chair or on the edge of your bed. Put the tennis ball on the floor and roll it around using the bottom of your foot.

Do this slowly, making sure you cover the whole underside of your foot. If you feel any tender areas - spend a bit more time on that point.

Spend some time doing this to the bottom of each of your feet.

This is a great way to relax your body – you can even do this while watching TV in the evening.

High Five Blaster for Nightmares...

The High Five Blaster is great to use when you have woken up from a nightmare and you feel yourself trapped in horrible thoughts.

The High Five set-up (do this during the day):

- Start by holding onto one of your thumbs it doesn't matter which hand you use.

- Now think about a time that makes you happy, that makes you smile. It could be a birthday, when you got a pet, doing well at something. It could be anything.

- Now hold onto your first finger and think of another happy time.

- Repeat, until you have thought of something happy for each of the five fingers on one hand.

Now, when you find yourself needing a mood boost you can focus on your hand and give yourself your own personal High Five.
Just start by holding your thumb and really thinking about that first happy memory, then move onto the next finger and the next.
When you have done all five then see how you feel.

You will find yourself feeling better.

Note:

You can alter the order of your happy memories.
You can also change the memories that you are using whenever you want to.
If you feel you need even more of a mood shift then you can add memories onto your other hand and make it a Big Ten Blaster.

You might find yourself lying in bed having woken up from a horrible dream, not wanting to close your eyes for fear of going back to it. This is a gentle way of getting your mind to shift to better thoughts.

Going to sleep...

This exercise will help your mind and body remember how to get to sleep. Just read through it, and give it a go.

- Lying in bed. Close your eyes.

- Notice how you are feeling. Are you grumpy, calm, stressed, happy, or sad.

- Imagine that you could scan through your body with your mind from the top of your head down to the soles of your feet, just notice how your body is feeling, which parts are comfortable or uncomfortable.

- Now work back up your body noticing each muscle and imagining it relaxing, your toes, feet, calves, stomach etc.

- Now you can start to focus on your breathing.

- Breathing deeply in and out of your nose, as if you could breathe into the depths of your stomach.

- When you next breathe out count 1, in your mind. Then count 2 on the next out-breath.

- Continue counting with each out-breath up to 10, and then start again with 1.

- Repeat.

Getting into the habit of doing this when you get into bed will help promote your new good sleep habit. Remember, even lying in bed just relaxing is good for your mind and body.

And finally...

Is something stressing you out?

Different things can affect your sleep. The most common issue that affects sleep is stress.

Stress can completely wreck your sleep.

This is why you see so many stressed out grumpy adults!

If you think you are suffering from stress look at Chapter 2 for more help.

*"No wonder Sleeping Beauty looked so good...
she took long naps, never got old, and didn't have to
do anything but snore to get her Prince Charming."*

Olive Green

SECTION 6
Fear, the Unwanted Visitor

What if it's there?

I'm afraid

Spiders

Lifts

I'm afraid to feel
that scared again

I can't cope

Thunder

Planes

I can't do
what I want

No one
understands

Dogs

Bees

I'm scared

Fear, the visiting alien...

The fear isn't you.

It isn't who you are.

You weren't born with this fear.

It can go away.

It is an unwanted guest that's outstayed its welcome.

It's time to see it off!

Fear is your brains way of looking after you...

It wants to keep you safe.

And it's doing a really good job!

Your brain believes that the thing you are afraid of, whatever it is - bees, thunder, balloons etc. is life threatening.

So its going to keep you away from it.

How?

By making you terrified.

Many people have something they are afraid of. But it's not something that people discuss so you probably won't know anyone else who is afraid of the same thing.

Read on if:

You are scared of something.

You are fed up of feeling scared.

You are scared of feeling scared and avoiding things and places.

You are fed up of this fear stopping you from doing what you want to do.

Rate that (Annoying) Fear...

Think right now about that thing you are scared of.

Take a moment - close your eyes and really think about it.

Rate where you feel you are on this scale:

10 - terrified

    9 - unbelievably scared

       8 - really scared

          7 - afraid

            6 - frightened

               5 - scared

            4 - nervous

          3 - worried

       2 - bit uncomfortable

    1 - not bothered

0 - Don't know, can't tell

Step 1 - Make Yourself a Film Star...

There are two ways you can do this - both will help shift that fear.

1. Think about a time in the past when you came face-to-face with the thing you fear.

2. Imagine a time in the future when you might have to face that fear.

Think about that time, in the past or in the future and create your film:

Look at a space on your wall.

Imagine there is a TV screen on it.

A film of you is now playing on the TV.

At the start of the film you see that you are calm and relaxed.

As you watch the film you see yourself coming face-to-face with your fear, either at some point in the past, or in your future.

That passes and at the end of the film you are once again safe and well.

The film stops.

Step 2:

1. Now imagine you can rewind the film, see everything happening backwards. You see yourself safe and well then going backwards through everything - until you are safe and well again (it is usually funny to imagine this). Now imagine watching the film all the way through again.

2. Take a moment to think of a song that makes you smile.

3. Now, once again imagine watching that film of you - but this time play that song, like a soundtrack to your film.

Doing this a few times will really make a difference to how you feel.

Tapping Away the Fear...

This will help your mind let go of that unwanted fear. Tapping will prepare the way for change.

Repeat this exercise a few times over a couple of days.

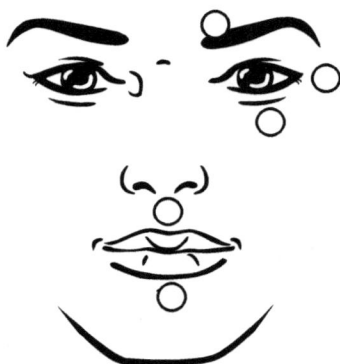

Tap 8 times on each point with two fingers while repeating the statement below over and over again:

Even though I am scared of _____, I am ok.

Finish by tapping all over the top of your head with your fingertips like raindrops.

Doing this exercise every couple of days, when you are at home, will really make a difference and will help you shift that unwanted alien.

Super Teddy's...

This is a great - if slightly bonkers way of getting that deeper part of your mind to sort out this fear for you. You don't even really need to know what's going on - just give it a go!

Sometimes it feels as though there is a battle going on in your mind - one part of your mind saying everything is ok while the other part wants you to run away.

This exercise will get those parts to work together.

1. Get two soft toys.

2. Sit somewhere comfortable - where you won't be disturbed.

3. Pick up one of the toys - imagine this is the part of you that is afraid.

4. Ask this toy why it wants you to be afraid. Ask it again and again until it runs out of answers. (Just imagine that it could answer you.)
   e.g. Why do you want me to be afraid of bees?
     - Because they are scary
     - They might sting
     - If you are scared you won't go outside
     - You will be safe inside and nothing will hurt you
     - You will be happy

5. Now, pick up the other toy.
   Imagine this is the part of you that wants to no longer be afraid.

6. Ask this toy why it wants you to stop being afraid. Ask it again and again until it runs out of answers.
   (Again imagine that it could answer you.)
   e.g. Why do you want me to stop being afraid of bees?
     - So you can go outside
     - So you can be with friends
     - Want to be normal
     - To be able to go on school trips
     - To be happy

Both of these parts are looking after you.

They want you to be happy.

- Now get the toys to face each other.

- Imagine they were having a quiet talk (you don't have to know what they are saying).

- Imagine that they could work things out - negotiate with each other.

- When you think they have had enough time to work things out and come to an agreement bring them together (group hug!)

(Told you this was bonkers!)

Keep the toys handy - just in case you need to get them to work things out in the future.

It is important to get those different parts of you to work together – instead of that constant battle – both parts want you to be safe and happy. You don't have to know what they say to each other.

Breathe Out That Fear...

You have made some progress moving down the fear scale as you have worked through the exercises.

This exercise can help to shift any final remaining feelings.

- Think about whatever it is that you are afraid of.

- Take some deep breaths.

- Put your hands together so that they make a space between them, as if you were going to fill them with water and take a drink.

- Now take in a deep breath - imagine that you can bring all your fear into that breath - and breathe out into the space in your hands.

- Now take in another deep breath open your hands as you breathe out onto them - blowing away all that fear.

- Shake your hands out.

This is a great exercise to do when you have been working on getting rid of that alien, but there still seems to be a bit of fear left – doing this will help you let it go.

High Five Blaster...

This is a very useful technique that you can use when you are out and about and feel that fear is beginning to bother you.

It is important to set it up at home, when you are feeling ok.

Setting up your High Five Blaster:

Start by holding onto one of your thumbs it doesn't matter which hand you use.

Now think about a time that makes you happy, that makes you smile. It could be a birthday, when you got a pet or when you did well at something. It could be anything.

Now hold onto your first finger and think of another happy time.

Repeat, until you have thought of something happy for each of the five fingers on one hand.

Now, if you ever start to feel scared you can use your High Five Blaster.

Just start by holding your thumb and really thinking about that first happy memory, then move onto the next finger and the next.

And the best bit is you can use this anywhere:

In school   At the airport   At the shops   Anywhere

And no-one will know what you are doing.

Note:

You can alter the order of your happy memories.

You can also change the memories that you are using whenever you want to. If you feel you need even more of a boost then you can add memories onto your other hand and make it a Big Ten Blaster.

This is a great technique, which will help you feel more confident allowing you to cope easily in previously scary situations. Each time you use it you will feel more and more confident.

Planted Feet...

You can use this technique if you are feeling afraid and want a quick and easy way to calm down.

Take a moment to really notice where your feet are on the ground.

Sense the weight of your feet on the floor.

Relax your shoulders down.

Notice your breathing.

Start to breathe deeply - into the depths of your stomach. So that your breathing moves your stomach in and out.

Repeat for 5-10 breaths.

When you have done this you will find you are feeling calmer and more in control.

This is a useful technique that you can use anywhere and no-one will know what you are doing.

Magic Fingers...

It might be that you are worried about coming face-to-face with your fear at some point in the future or you might be facing your fear today.

What can you do when you feel that feeling of fear starting?

You can use acupressure points on your hand to calm you.

Your set-up:

Rate your feeling of fear between 1 and 10.

With your thumb and first finger squeeze the fingers of your other hand on opposite sides of each nail.

Starting with your thumb and squeeze each finger in turn.

Repeat on the other hand.

Breathing deeply while you do this.

Again rate your feeling of fear between 1 and 10.

You can do this as many times as you need to.

This exercise is great on its own – but even more powerful if used in combination with Planted Feet. This will also help if you have a fear of the fear – when you become scared of feeling afraid again.

Tapping into Calm...

You have made a lot of progress and now feel that the visiting alien of fear is on its way out. Tapping through this exercise will help your mind to let go of any final attachments to that old outdated fear.

Tap 8 times on each point with two fingers while repeating the statement below over and over again:

I can now let myself feel calm
when I think about _____, I am ok.

Finish by tapping with your fingertips all over the top of your head like raindrops.

This exercise will help reinforce the progress you have made with the other exercises in this chapter.

Ladder Challenge...

So, you have worked through the exercises, you have your calming techniques - now it's time for you to build up your confidence in yourself. It's time to take on the Ladder Challenge!

Imagine you are going up a ladder and it has 10 steps - the top step represents how you want to feel. You are starting at the bottom.

Think about whatever it is that you are afraid of, for example spiders. What is the least scary thing to do with spiders you can think of? It could be looking at a spider in the garden through a window.

Step 1:

Now imagine looking at that spider through a window. Use the skills you have learnt to calm any small feelings of fear you may have. Like planted feet, magic fingers etc.

Step 2:

What is the next thing you could now just about think of doing?

Possibly looking at a spider from a long way away.

Again use your calming techniques, and breathing to lower any feelings of fear.

Repeat this and go up another step on your ladder. Keep going.

Each time you move on a step you should feel completely calm and relaxed, if there are any nerves then you should stay on that step a while longer.

This is a really important challenge – as you do this you will build up trust in yourself and feel more confident and able to cope.

Now once again...

Rate that Fear...

How scared are you?

I want you to think right now about the thing that you are scared of.

Rate where you think you now are on this scale:

10 - terrified

    9 - unbelievably scared

        8 - really scared

            7 - afraid

                6 - frightened

                    5 - scared

                4 - nervous

            3 - worried

        2 - bit uncomfortable

    1 - not bothered

0 - Don't know - can't tell

Wherever you are on this scale you will find that there has been an improvement. Keep practicing the techniques until you find yourself just where you want to be.

Now get out there and test that change!

I know you might be afraid of feeling the fear again - but you need to know that there will have been a change and the only way that you are going to find this out is to test it.

Go on

Off you go

Get out

Now

Go on!

*"Becoming fearless isn't the point.
That's impossible. It's learning how
to control your fear, and how to be free from it."*

Veronica Roth

SECTION 7
Coping with School

I'm nervous

Work

I worry
about school

My Stomach
hurts

Corridors

Teachers

I feel
stressed out

I can't eat

Meeting
new people

Walking into class

I feel like crying
all the time

School is making me worried

School

School can sometimes be stressful.

The school you are in might be making you stressed.

Or, you might be starting a new school.

Parents forget what it was like...

Remember they went to school in the Stone Age; they have no idea of what life is like now.

They don't know how to dress, how to look or how to fit in. (They didn't even have mobile phones then!)

In this section I am going to teach you some skills that will help you cope and feel more confident.

How are school worries affecting you?

Sleep

School can make you anxious, which
can mess up your sleep.
You might have trouble getting to sleep.
You might find you wake in the night and find it
hard to get back to sleep.

Stomach-aches

School stress can mess up your stomach.
It might ache, or feel like it is in knots.
You might find yourself running to the toilet.

Tears

When you are anxious and worried
you can feel tearful all the time.
Bursting into tears at the drop of a hat is
not good in high school.

Lack of Confidence

At your old school you knew where you were,
you knew the teachers, you had friends and you felt safe.
A new school can shake your confidence.
You need a way to boost your confidence.

Worry about making new friends

You might be worried about making new friends.
Constant worry can make you feel tired and ill.
Feeling lonely can make you low and sad.

Something Happened in School - Tapping Yourself Free...

Sometimes something happened at school and even though it's in the past it might still be making you feel anxious about school.

This exercise will help you to let go of those feelings.

Tap 8 times on each point with two fingers while repeating the statement below over and over again:

Something happened in school that made me feel anxious, I am ok now.

Finally tap all over the top of your head with your fingertips like rain drops.

Going through this exercise a few times will help your mind let go of that anxious memory.

The ABBA Effect...

Is there a specific event from the past at school that is still bothering you?

Perhaps someone said something mean to you.
Perhaps a teacher embarrassed you.

Whatever it is - doing this exercise will release its hold over you.

Using the ABBA Effect:

Close your eyes.

Think of the event.

Now think of an ABBA song.

Play the song in your mind as you think about the event.

Imagine you could put a picture frame around the event - with glittering lights on the frame - now play the music in your head.

Close your eyes and really imagine it.

This is great to use on an embarrassing event that still makes you feel awful. Doing this will take away its power over you.

A Day in School - a Film of You...

Getting your mind to go through your school day can help it to deal with any fears or worries about school. Do this exercise as many times as you feel you need to.

You might find it helpful to close your eyes, or to stare at a blank space on the wall in front of you.

Imagine there is a TV in front of you.

Playing on this TV is a film of your normal school day.

Imagine that you could see yourself getting ready for school.

See yourself going to school and starting your day.

Now you can imagine that you see everything going well, imagine where you are, see the people around you.

Everything goes just as you would like it to, you go to your different lessons, have lunch, see your friends.

You feel good, look happy, confident.

You return home, happy, it went well and you are smiling and feeling good.

When your mind imagines something over and over it begins to believe that it can happen that way – and it will make it happen as you imagine it. Top athletes use this technique.

Magic Fingers...

Use this technique when you feel anxious at school - it will calm you down, and no one will know you are doing it.

Each of your fingers has acupressure points on it, which can help calm your emotions.

- Squeeze each finger on one hand, squeezing on either side of each nail.

- Start with your thumb, finishing with your little finger.

- Take some deep breaths while doing this.

You can do this as many times as you need to.

This is a useful technique to use when you are feeling a bit anxious, perhaps before you have to speak in front of people.

Creating Your Own Confidence Booster...

This is a fantastic way of giving your confidence a boost. It can help when you need a boost in confidence to go up and talk to a group of friends, or a teacher.

Setting up your confidence booster:

- Think about a time when you felt good. It could be - the day you did well in a spelling test, when you scored a goal, the day you got something you really wanted.

- Close your eyes and really think about that moment - where you were, how you felt, feel that good feeling growing inside of you. Imagine you were there again, right now.

- Clench your hands into fists and hold that good feeling, allow it to grow stronger inside you.

Repeat to strengthen your booster.

You can even add another memory to make your confidence booster even more powerful.

Now when you need a confidence boost just clench your hands and feel that good feeling flow through you blasting confidence into every part of you.

You can set up your confidence booster at home – then use it whenever you want – if you need a boost to walk into a classroom then this will help you.

Planted Feet...

This will help calm your nerves, wherever you are.

- Take a moment to really notice where your feet are on the ground.

- Really feel the weight of your feet on the ground.

- Relax your shoulders.

- Notice your breathing.

- Start to breathe deeply - into the depths of your stomach. So that your breathing moves your stomach in and out.

- Continue for as long as you need to.

You can use this exercise in school to help you feel calmer.

This is a wonderful technique that can help you find calm and balance and the best thing is no-one will know that you are doing it.

Have something in your life other than school...

If school is the only thing in your life and it's not going well then this will have a huge impact on your life - making you miserable.

When you have other things going on in your life like guides, scouts, drama club, dance etc. then this lowers the importance of school and makes life easier.

SECTION 8
Exams and Tests

Exams make
me nervous

What if I fail?

I can't think
straight

Exams

Math

I don't know
anything

I feel sick

Mocks

Science

Everyone else
is writing

Finals

Exams - help!

Testing, testing, testing...

Some days it seems like there are a never-ending number of exams and tests.

**You can't avoid exams so it will make your life
easier if you learn how to cope with them.**

Working through the exercises and learning the skills in this chapter will help you be calmer during exams, have a clearer mind and get better grades.

The Golden Rules of Exams:

1. Check both sides of the question paper.

2. Give questions the right amount of time based on the marks they are worth - if you get stuck MOVE ON.

3. If you have spare time at the end - use it and read through everything you have written, it might be boring - but you might gain a couple of marks which may make the difference to your grade.

4. And finally;

Revise, revise, revise.

These are the golden rules - do this and you will be on your way to getting good grades.

They might not be that exciting but if you follow these rules you will find you get better marks.

Revising ... well!

Ok, I am going to give it to you straight - there are no short cuts for revision.

Revision is a skill that you can learn.

How to revise well:

- Time - start early, avoid the stress of last minute revision.

- No Sound - it uses up important parts of your brain - if you really want to remember everything you need to have quiet so you can focus.

- Write it out - write out the notes you are trying to learn - in full, in pen (no computers allowed!). Do this three times - on different days.

- Write out key points or equations - write these over and over and over, repeating them out loud as you do this. This helps the information stick in your memory in different ways.

- Use past exam papers - as this will help you learn how they are going to phrase the questions. Each exam has its own style of wording, and its own ways that the questions will try and trick you. Learn these tricks and you will boost your grades.

It is important to learn how to revise.

There are no short cuts.

You have to put the time in.

Sorry! I know you were hoping for a short cut – but there just aren't any!

Tapping out Exam Worries...

You might have found an exam difficult in the past, and thinking about it might still make you feel upset - this exercise will help your mind let go of that memory and prepare the way for doing well in the future.

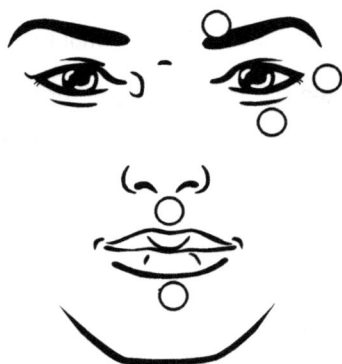

Tap 8 times on each point with two fingers while repeating the statement below over and over again:

Even though I found that exam _____ I am ok.

Finish by tapping all over the top of your head, like raindrops, with your fingertips.

This will help you to let go of any worries about past exams and allow you to move on to a more positive future.

Helping Your Brain Learn...

How can you trick your mind into remembering more?

Change the font!

The harder a font is to read the more you will remember.

So if you have something that you really need to learn -

Change the font!

This is a really useful technique if you have, for example, a poem that you need to learn – type it into your computer and print it out in a strange font. You will find learning and remembering the poem much easier.

Help, More Brain Power Needed!

Sometimes when you are revising your brain feels like it needs a boost of energy - Try this it will activate your brain energy!

Sit somewhere comfortable.

Become aware of your breathing and breathe deeply and slowly.

Place your thumbs on your temples and your fingers on the center of your forehead.

Begin to slowly pull your fingers apart moving towards your temples, gently stretching the skin on your forehead.

Repeat this process over the front, middle and back of your head.

Finally pulling your fingers down your neck to your shoulders and let your hands drop. Breathing deeply.

Now, tap all over the top of your head, like raindrops.

This exercise gives you an instant energy boost and a two minute revision break – your brain will then be ready to learn more!

Planted Feet...

You can use this when you are standing waiting to go into the exam hall, or when you are sitting at the desk and need to calm your mind.

It will also work well at home when you are revising and you need to calm your mind and increase your focus.

- Take a moment to really notice where your feet are on the ground.

- Sense the weight of your feet on the ground.

- Become aware of your shoulders; just let them gently relax away from your ears.

- Make sure your jaw is relaxed.

- Notice your breathing.

- Start to breathe deeply - into the depths of your stomach. So that your breathing moves your stomach in and out.

Do this for a minute and you will find yourself feeling calmer and clearer.

This is a useful exercise to do when you are surrounded by all your friends who are jabbering and building up their nerves. This exercise will calm you and help you to be focused and feel in control.

Your Pre-Exam Routine...

This is a great routine to do at home before leaving for your exam. The acupressure points will help calm your nerves and also boost your memory.

Pre-Exam Routine

Start by taking some deep breaths into your belly.

Press the area just under the points of your collarbone; gently press both sides with the fingertips of each hand. Hold for five deep belly breaths.

Turn one of your hands to face you, following the creases on your wrist to the edge gently press the area directly under your little finger with the thumb of your other hand. Hold this point for 3 deep belly breaths.

Now place a finger on the center of your wrist crease and measure 3 finger widths towards your elbow. Press and hold this point for three deep belly breaths.

This is a very quick routine, which you can do before leaving for your exam. It has a calming effect and will help calm your mind.

Increase Your Focus...

Sometimes when you are sat in the exam hall it can be hard to maintain your concentration.

You might find your mind wandering, drifting away from what you are meant to be doing.

Doing this simple exercise will help maintain your focus on the exam paper.

- Relax your jaw.

- Place the tip of your tongue on the roof of your mouth, just behind your front teeth (and keep it there!)

- You will find that your mind instantly becomes more focused.

This is a strange but effective technique, which really helps your focus.

Easy Memory Trick - 1...

Left nostril breathing - This is a bonkers trick!

It has been shown that when you hold your right nostril shut and breathe slowly through your left nostril that your memory is improved.
(And no one knows why!)

A trick you can use when you need a memory boost during your exam!

Stuck on a question during the exam – try a quick bit of left nostril breathing and see if your brain can come up with the answer!

Easy Memory Trick - 2...

Chewing gum - This is another bonkers trick!

When you chew gum you have a better memory.

Another trick you can use when you need a memory boost during your exam!

If your school has banned chewing gum this might be one trick you need to avoid!

High Five Blaster...

You might find that negative exam worries are taking over your thoughts - this technique will help shift them.

Set up your High Five Blaster:

Start by holding onto one of your thumbs it doesn't matter which hand you use.

Now think about a time that makes you happy, that makes you smile. It could be a birthday, when you got a pet, doing well at something. It could be anything.

Now hold onto your first finger and think of another happy time.

Repeat, until you have thought of something happy for each of the five fingers on one hand.

Now, when you find yourself needing to blast away those negative exam thoughts you can give yourself your own personal High Five.

Just start by holding your thumb and really thinking about that first happy memory, then move on to the next finger and the next.

When you have done all five - **You will feel better.**

And the best bit is you can use this anywhere - even in an exam hall.

Note:

You can alter the order of your happy memories. You can also change the memories that you are using whenever you want to. If you feel you need even more of a boost then you can add memories onto your other hand and make it a Big Ten Blaster.

Sometimes, especially if you have a big exam coming up, you will feel your worries and negative thoughts building up. Doing this exercise will help you reduce your worries and feel more positive. When your mind is full of positive thoughts there is no space for worries.

Emergency Calmer...

You might find yourself sitting in the exam feeling stressed out. Wondering how you are going to get through it.

This powerful technique lowers stress and promotes a feeling of calm.

- Press the area of skin between your thumb and first finger with the thumb and first finger of your other hand.

- Hold for up to a minute.

- Change sides and repeat.

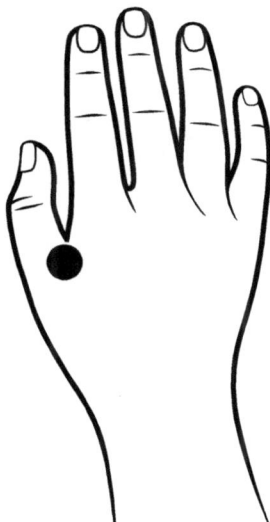

This is a widely used technique for lowering stress levels.
Do not teach this to anyone who is pregnant.

And finally...

Try not to talk to people before the exam .... Nerves are catching and you don't need to know what other people have or haven't done.

And later ..... don't dissect the paper with friends - it will only set up worries.

Keep your calm and you will keep your focus.

SECTION 9
Trips and Sleepovers

School Trips

I worry
at night

I miss
my family

I don't
feel safe

Scout Camp

Sleepovers

I can't sleep

What if I go,
and I'm upset

I'm nervous about
going away

Guide camp

I want to go, but I don't want to go - help!

Being homesick is rubbish...

It just seems to take over your brain and the only way that you can imagine ever feeling any better is to be at home, safe and well.

It also seems that as you get older there are more and more trips away from home.

You might feel:

It was ok going away last year - but it's not ok now.

I've never liked staying away from home.

I want to be able to forget about home while I am away and have fun.

I don't want to miss out.

You can learn how to help yourself enjoy sleepovers and trips away from home.

Imagine how good would it feel to be able to enjoy being with your friends on trips.

That is just what this section is going to help you be able to do.

Homesickness is your brains way of looking after you...

What?

Your brain is always trying to look after you.

It is your brains job to keep you safe, well and alive at all times.

When you feel homesick you might be away on something like a school trip, at a friend's, or on a guide or scout camp.

You are doing something new or different this can make you feel a bit nervous.

Your brain can register this nervous feeling as one of DANGER.

And it wants to keep you away from DANGER - so it makes you want to go home more than anything.

Your brain wants you to be safe.

Time to Retrain Your Brain...

You are going to teach your brain that feeling nervous can be a good thing.

It means that your world is getting bigger - you are discovering new things.

It means you are doing something new and new can be good.

You need to retrain your brain!

You need to teach your brain that you are now a teenager.

You can cope with some excitement.

You can enjoy new situations.

How are you going to do this?

By going through the exercises in this section you will start to retrain your brain and you will also learn some easy calming techniques that will help you when you are away from home.

The Waves of Homesickness...

The feelings of homesickness come along like waves.

This means that the feelings will be really strong for a moment and then seem to drop down into nothing, before building up again.

You can learn how to cope with the peak of the homesickness wave.

This leaves you to have some fun as those feelings die down.

As you learn to cope you will find the peaks become smaller and smaller and easier and easier to deal with.

Learn to surf the waves.

Tapping Free of Homesickness...

Doing this exercise a couple of times, on different days, before you go away will help you break down that feeling of homesickness.

Tap 8 times on each point with two fingers while repeating the statement below over and over again:

Even though I have been homesick in the past, I am ok now.

Finish by tapping all over the top of your head, like raindrops, with your fingertips.

You might have tried a few times to stay away from home and found yourself feeling homesick – this exercise will help your mind break free of that negative habit.

Time Travel...

Read through this then give it a go:

Close your eyes and; Imagine you are staying somewhere away from home for the night.

You find yourself feeling like you want to go home, let that feeling grow stronger and stronger.

Now, imagine each of these outcomes:

1. **You go home early** - it's a week later, how do you feel about the fact that you went home? How do you feel when you hear people discussing the trip? The things they did, the fun they had. Close your eyes and really focus on how that makes you feel.

2. **You stay** - It's now a week later and you are chatting with friends about all the things you did. You feel happy, proud of yourself - part of the group.

Again, close your eyes and imagine how good that would feel. Clap your hands now - really loudly.

Do this exercise a few days before you are due to go away. It will help your mind imagine another, better, alternative. And when you are away it will remind you of the positive reasons for staying.

The reality of home -

It can be boring.

It's usually a lot more fun being away with friends!

Making your life longer...

How can you make your life longer?

Think about the last time you went somewhere new for the weekend, it might have been with your family.

That weekend felt so long, think about all the things you packed into it - and when you got back it felt as though you had been away for ages - not just two days.

Now, think about last weekend, a normal 'at home' weekend. It seemed to rush by, and in what seemed like only a few hours you found yourself back in school.

So, you can make your life longer.

Going away - doing new things makes your life seem longer!

Think about this the next time you are invited to go somewhere – do you want your life to zoom by – or do you want to pack as much into it as possible?

Tapping out the Fear
of it happening again...

You might find yourself worried about going away - just in case those feelings come back - do this exercise a couple of times on different days before you go away and it will help you let go of those feelings.

Tap 8 times on each point with two fingers while repeating the statement below over and over again:

Even though I am worried about
feeling homesick again, I am ok.

Finish by tapping all over the top of your head, like raindrops, with your fingertips.

This will help you feel calmer and to know that you can trust yourself and enjoy going away.

Your Trip on Film...

Prepare yourself for a good trip away from home by imagining how it will go.

You might find it helpful to close your eyes, or to stare at a blank space on the wall in front of you.

Imagine there is a TV in front of you.

Playing on this TV is a film of your trip away.

Imagine that you could see yourself getting ready to go, packing, looking happy.

See yourself going to meet the people you are going with. You say goodbye to your family. You are excited to be going.

Imagine you could see yourself arriving, finding out where you will be sleeping. Enjoying yourself.

The trip is going well, you are having fun.

You feel good, look happy and confident.

You return home, happy, it went well and you see yourself smiling and feeling good.

When your mind imagines something over and over it begins to believe that it can happen that way – and it will make it happen as you imagine it. This is why top athletes use this technique.

Calming down...

There you are far away from home and you feel a tingling of homesickness starting up. **Don't Panic** - these pressure points will calm that feeling down.

Take some deep belly breaths.

Turn one hand to face you, palm side up. Now, using your thumb, gently press the center of your wrist crease. Hold for five deep breaths.

Slide your thumb over to the edge of your hand, directly under your little finger (in between the two bones) and gently press this point for five deep breaths.

Finally, hold the area of skin between your thumb and first finger between the thumb and first finger of your other hand. Hold this point for about a minute. See page 133.

Taking just a quiet moment to do this will help you calm down and allow you to enjoy being away.

Sleeping Somewhere New - Help!

Ok, you are lying there:

Eyes open
Listening for new sounds
Listening to others sleeping
It feels like you are the only one awake

Help!

Here is what you can do - (read through this before you go so you know what to do) - and the best bit is - it's easy!

Take a deep breath in and look up.

As you breathe out close your eyes.

Breathe in and open your eyes, looking up.

Breathe out - close your eyes.

Repeat this about 10 times (you don't have to count just do it a load of times).

On the last time leave your eyes closed.

Now imagine you could be aware of each bit of your body - just taking a moment to scan through each bit of your entire body as you lie there.

Starting with your toes and feet - relax the muscles.

Calves - relax, thighs, stomach, relax.

Working through all the muscles in your body relaxing each in turn - finishing at the top of your head.

Now slowly breathe deeply in and out 10 times, breathing into the very depths of your stomach.

Let your thoughts drift off so that you start thinking about a happy place.

It's a good idea to try this out before you go away.

Magic Fingers...

There are acupressure points on your hands, which will help ease, any anxious feelings. This technique is easy to use when you are away and you find yourself feeling just a bit worried.

Helping you to feel better when you are away.

Your set-up:

Rate how worried you are between 1 and 10.

With your thumb and first finger squeeze the fingers of your other hand on opposite sides of each nail.

Starting with your thumb and squeeze each finger in turn.

Repeat on the other hand.

Breathing deeply while you do this.

Again rate how worried you are now between 1 and 10, you will find things have improved.

You can do this as many times as you need to.

This will help you ease any feelings of anxiousness. You can even use this technique on your way there.

Planted Feet...

This is a great exercise that you can use anywhere. It easily calms anxious feelings. Lowering anxiety will allow you to surf the wave of homesickness.

- Take a moment to really notice where your feet are on the ground, sitting or standing.

- Feel the weight of your feet on the ground.

- Notice your shoulders; just let them gently relax away from your ears.

- Start to breathe deeply - into the depths of your stomach. So that your breathing moves your stomach in and out. Repeat for a few breaths.

When you feel more confident in your ability to ease any feelings of homesickness then you will start to enjoy yourself more. Each time you use this technique you will feel more and more confident – and will need to use it less and less.

Remember...

You might just have fun!

Acknowledgements...

I would like to thank all the teenagers I have worked with. Your desire to change and improve your life, and willingness to let me help you is constantly inspiring.

I would also like to thank my own teenage daughters, Rosie and Molly - who sometimes ask for help, and occasionally listen! In return they have taught me a huge amount about life.

About the Author...

Kimberly Willis is a therapist, mother, wife and dog owner.

She is based in Sheffield, UK, where just occasionally there is sunshine, although not so far this year.

Before becoming a therapist Kimberly gained a PhD in Chemistry, this knowledge is now put to good use in helping her teens with their homework. This is her second book.

Her first book, The Little Book of Diet Help, has been published in over 11 countries.

www.kimberlywillis.co.uk